AF255465

Valor to Live

"There is but one truly serious philosophical problem,
and that is suicide!"

Albert Camus

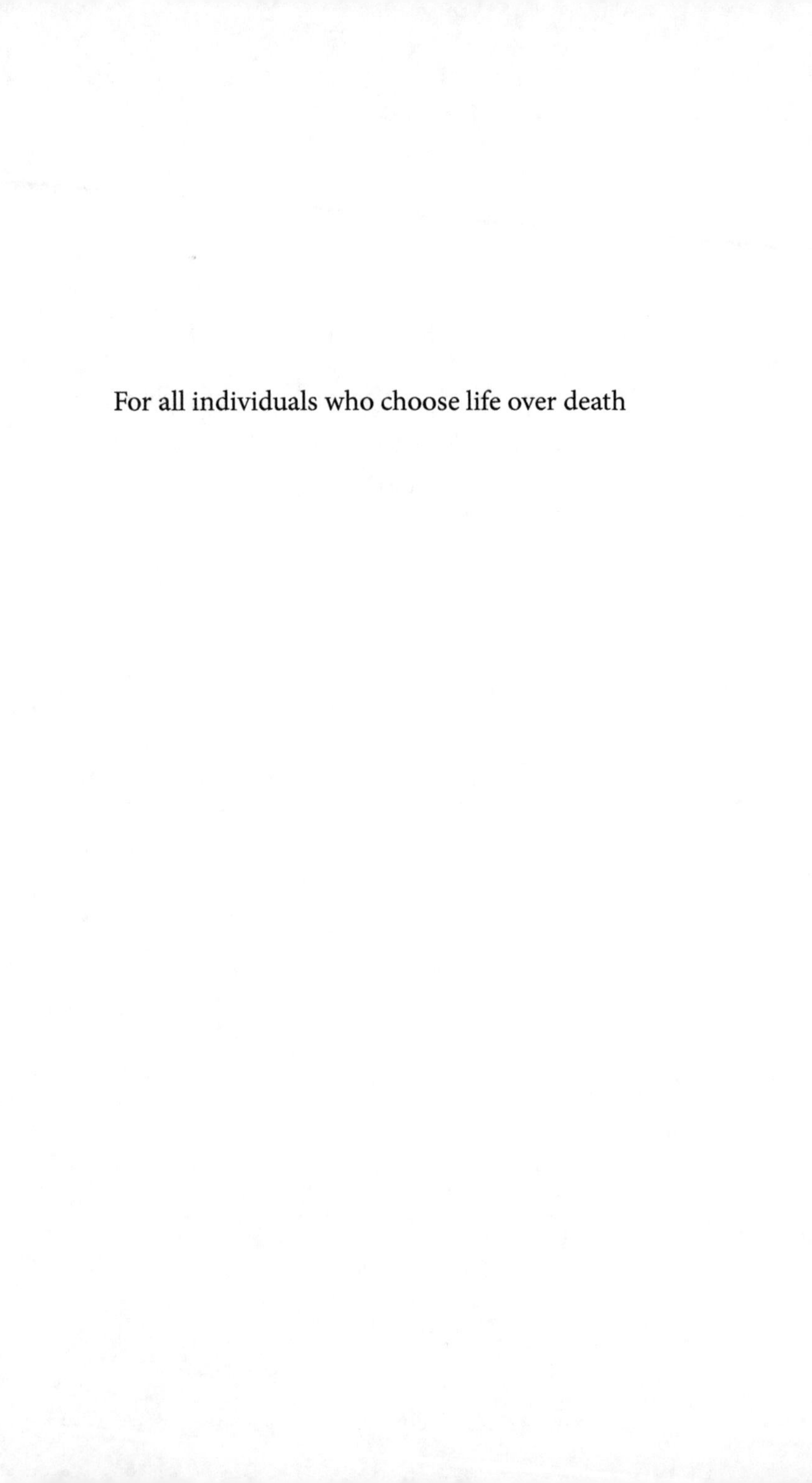

For all individuals who choose life over death

VALOR TO LIVE
Beyond Despair

Resource Publications
An Imprint of Wipf and Stock Publishers
199 W. 8th Ave., Suite 3
Eugene, OR 97401

www.wipfandstock.com

PAPERBACK ISBN: 978-1-6667-8134-2
HARDCOVER ISBN: 978-1-6667-8135-9
EBOOK ISBN: 978-1-6667-8136-6

VERSION NUMBER 070623

Valor to Live

Beyond Despair

DAVID H. ROSEN, M.D.

Foreword by
Nathan Mascaro, Ph.D.

RESOURCE *Publications* · Eugene, Oregon

Foreword

When reading this work, it might prove useful to keep in mind the mythic way of thinking and the capacity for connecting to more powerful Truths when engaging the mythic mindset. When I co-taught Psychology of Religion with Dr. David Rosen in 2003 at Texas A&M University, I noticed that he teaches each religion from its own perspective, and he believes.

Here David will summarize his own personal myth, hinging on a concept he calls egocide. In many cases egocide is generated by depressive emotions that (if properly interpreted) motivate decisions to subvert a part of oneself that poses as—is under the illusion it is—the Self. This rather than allowing depression to lead to actual Self killing. Dr. Rosen discusses his own process (and that of some patients of this good-humored psychiatrist), which involves artistic expression flowing from a combination of emotional pain and the sense of liberation generated by releasing attachments to personae that individuals have allowed to define or essentialize themselves for too long.

Since meeting him as one of his graduate students in 2000, I've been privileged to witness David's continuing egocide, which is truly a playful process, but also a powerfully energized one. This concept has been integral in his treatment of countless patients, training of countless clinicians, loving powerfully his family and friends, creating numerous works of artistic and psychological expression, and manifesting joy from the Self that breathes through him and all of us.

Commit egocide, not suicide. And let the sacrificed ego serve as fertile ground in which the heart will grow and blossom.

Nathan Mascaro, Ph.D.

Acknowledgement

This is in memory of the late June Singer...an exceptional human being, author, and Jungian analyst. To all the brave people that I saw in consultation who had made attempts to end their lives, but chose to live. I worked with these people in individual therapy and in a special group for serious sucide attempters. Both individual and group therapies were successful. I thank Alex Weston, James Miller Jr., and Nick Denning for their assistance. Also, a heartfelt thanks to Nathan Mascaro for his foreword. In addition, I deeply appreciate the support of Lanara Rosen.

Preface

The critical aspect of life is to be your true self. That is achieved by realizing your own personal myth. Your personal myth is the discovery and fulfillment of your unique purpose in being on this earth.

This book concerns having the valor to live beyond despair. It involves overcoming and finding meaning in ones depression.

The most personal setbacks are the most important lessons. This book is the result of a lifetime search and research into depression, melancholia and suicidology. In the reference section, I've listed some articles and a book that I either have authored or co- authored regarding this critical enigma. For example, it is the basis for the volume "Transforming Depression: Healing the Soul through Creativity," which was originally published in 1993 and is still in print. It is based on my experiences, writings and findings regarding suicidal depression. I shared a draft of this material with the late June Singer. She was a supervisor and friend of mine as well as the author of several books including "Boundaries of the Soul," which was an early glimpse into the world of C. G. Jung.

"Valor to Live" is for everyone who has struggled with thoughts or attempts to end their life. Ego equals "I" and represents the personal self. Whereas the Self is the center in totality of being. Hence, the term egocide is a meaningful alternative to suicide. Egocide allows suicidal individuals to keep living and fulfill their personal myths. I shared the book material with June Singer, and she wanted me to call "Transforming Depression," "Read This Book Before You Commit Suicide," but Putnam, the publisher, said no. It was too provocative. They wanted a more general title that would apply to depression, the most common mental disorder. I went with Putnam's suggestion. The energy that goes into self-destruction should be channeled into self-construction. What I mean by this is, no one really wants to end their life. This is the basis for all treatment to prevent suicide. Often people fail at something and they then feel they are a failure. The person feels hopeless, however, there is always hope. Hope just needs to be rediscovered. When I was in medical school, I decided to paint my way out of suicidal depression. In 1967 a book that had just been published, "Shamanism: The beginnings of Art," by Andreas Lommel, outlined a similar procedure. The shaman, who was often depressed, created things such as paintings. They would share them with the community, as a way of self healing. This book underscored a process similar to the one I had undergone. In other words, what I had experienced was validated in that book. It became a hallmark of my own approach to helping others with this deadly condition.

When I attended Whittier College, back in 1964, I met my first wife. She was a performing actress. After we met and spent some time together, we fell in love and wanted to get married. My parents objected to that idea basing their disapproval on the simple fact that they felt I was too young, being 19 years old. Despite their concerns, I married her anyway. I subsequently transferred to UC Berkeley with my new wife in tow. I studied pre-med and managed to maintain an average GPA of 3.25. I then attended medical school at the University of Missouri, in Columbia. Sadly my parents divorced during this time. My father remained in Springfield, Missouri. Whereas my mother took me and my siblings to California. This afforded me dual in state residency status.

I painted this piece in 1967, after my first year in medical school. It was difficult and depressing to learn from working on a dead human being. It was arduous learning gross anatomy as one must incorporate the use of 10,000 new words within the first year. This painting represents my inner feelings. It was clear that I was melancholic yet my personal theory was that there was substantive value in this condition. When I initially created this painting, I saw it's stormy nature, with mountains to climb and the sun in the sky representing that things would turn for the better. Reflecting back on it now, I feel the mountains represent the challenges of medical school, the dark waters at it's base, the constant feelings of turmoil and unrest dealing with the everyday challenges associated with medicine. The tower represents the pinnacle of achievement when I would graduate from medical school. The yellow sun represents an increasingly bright future and a burning desire to achieve.

While I was an intern at San Francisco General Hospital, I witnessed very stressful and shocking situations. Some of these real life tragedies involved treating gun shot victims, mutilations, stabbings and people involved in motor vehicle accidents. During this time, I had a patient named Robin who had experienced suicidal behavior. She was a talented young artist and was using art and painting to heal herself. I saw how our situations paralleled and it later evolved into one of the cornerstones of my medical practice. Her experience coupled with others helped me to write the book "Transforming Depression". In addition to my own experiences, in that book, I discuss four patients and reveal their artwork which enabled them to live fully.

Now I will briefly discuss two additional cases which are featured in the book, "Transforming Depression." One case was an adopted and depressed young man named Gary. He wanted a stable relationship with a woman and to find his mother, as well as to be a race car driver. Because of unrelenting pressure from his family members, he had not yet realized his dreams. Gary seemed to resemble a college aged student rather than a seasoned educator. I mention this to say, his youthful appearance seemed to mask his professional demeanor. Gary was a thirty-five year old, married man, who was an accomplished dancer, choreographer and college instructor. He met his wife, who was also a dancer, during his collegiate days. However, she was a problematic drinker and contributed to his initial spiral into depression. Gary's adoption contributed to his feelings of abandonment and added to his depression. He sought therapy to assist with his growing mental issues. During our sessions, he was able to communicate his displeasure about his wife's alcohol consumption which helped her eventually reducing the over all indulgence of alcohol. Gary seemed depressed about his unfulfilled desire to become a race car driver. With no family support and the daily pressures of providing for himself and his wife, there seemed to be no room for any encouragement to pursue one of his true passions. During his in-depth psychotherapy, which involved dream analysis, he presented this dream: He was upstairs in an attic loft, within a house, in the town where he went to college. An occult group meeting was in progress at this house, and he believed his wife was also there. Gary attempts to find her while confronting some of the members. He was engulfed with a sense of danger, then hears music and notices the members beginning to dance. Suddenly the room clears, then he spots and cuddles his female dog. Then he transforms into a young girl around the age of 6, and the dog disappears and she is left embracing herself.

Another dream, towards the end of his therapy, consisted of him being in a troubled and dangerous situation. Gary found himself walking through a room of sleeping snakes and a primitive ape. He was in the center of the room, unable to get out. Then a tall African American woman, in her early forties, leaps into the middle of the room and began to comfort him. She smiled, then leads him thru the snakes, past the ape and out of the room. Gary then felt safe.

The serpent is a well substantiated healing symbol. In this dream, the female represents a healing anima, which is the feminine nature of a man's psyche which guides him through the dangers. Then he could continue his process of individuation or journey to wholeness. As we delved into the first dream, he expressed that he once was fascinated by the occult. He also stated, while in college he dated a woman who was a Wiccan.

Gary longed to find his biological mother and in his dream when he sought out his wife, he could just as well have been seeking his birth mother. In therapy we explored the unconditional love received from his female dog, and the young girl eventually embracing herself representing his own self love. All the female imagery, seemed to point to him finding his inner feminine nature or anima. While improving his marital relationship and searching for and being reunited with his biological mother, he eventually felt his depressive issues vastly lessened, thereby affording him the ability to leave therapy.

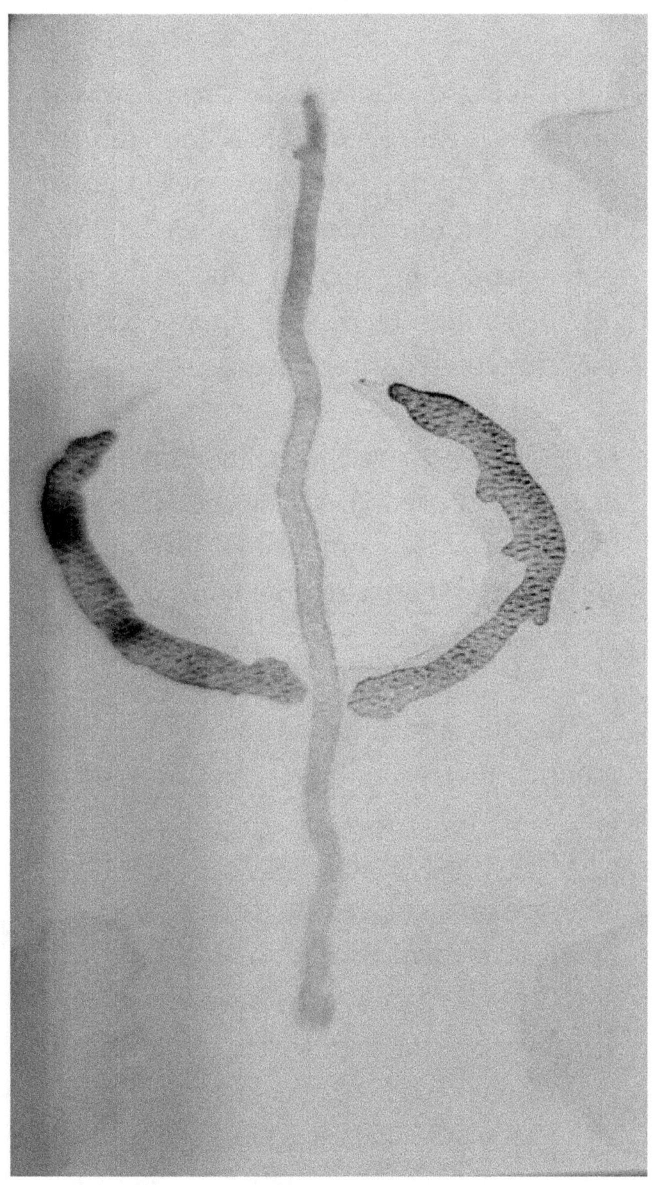

I encouraged Gary to express himself through creative art. He chose to paint and his his painting above shows two snakes, one red and one blue. The red snake illustrates masculinity and the blue snake represents femininity. By tying them together, they represented wholeness.

I often follow up with my patients after they have left my care. He did well and grew to like himself. He continued in his work as an educator and choreographer but was no longer performing or did administrative tasks. He became a professional race car driving instructor during the summer months, thereby fulfilling another goal of his.

Another case involved a twenty-six year old graduate student named Sharon. She suffered from self-destructive depression and a history of suicidal attempts. In addition, she had very low self esteem and body image. She was separated from her husband, a college professor, who acted as a father figure. However, he along with her family, championed and encouraged her high intellectual achievements. They supported her in achieving a Ph.D. Ironically, she berated herself for not receiving all A's. Despite making excellent grades, she became withdrawn and drank alcohol for comfort. Her parents wanted a male child to take over the family business, being that they had no sons and Sharon was the eldest of two daughters, it fell upon her shoulders to fulfill those expectations. Sharon had her own ideas for her future. After several months in therapy, she recounted a dream that her and her husband planned to destroy where they were living, with a nuclear device. Her dream analysis determined that staying with her husband would have meant her own destruction. Sharon also dreamt her parents died in a plane crash. In a way, she felt like a parentless child. This represented her being on her own. Sharon's dream expressed a need to become her own self by detaching from her parents expectations.

She marveled at the healing aspect of psychotherapy and analysis. She then considered becoming an analyst, which she later realized. Sharon eventually divorced her husband and moved abroad.

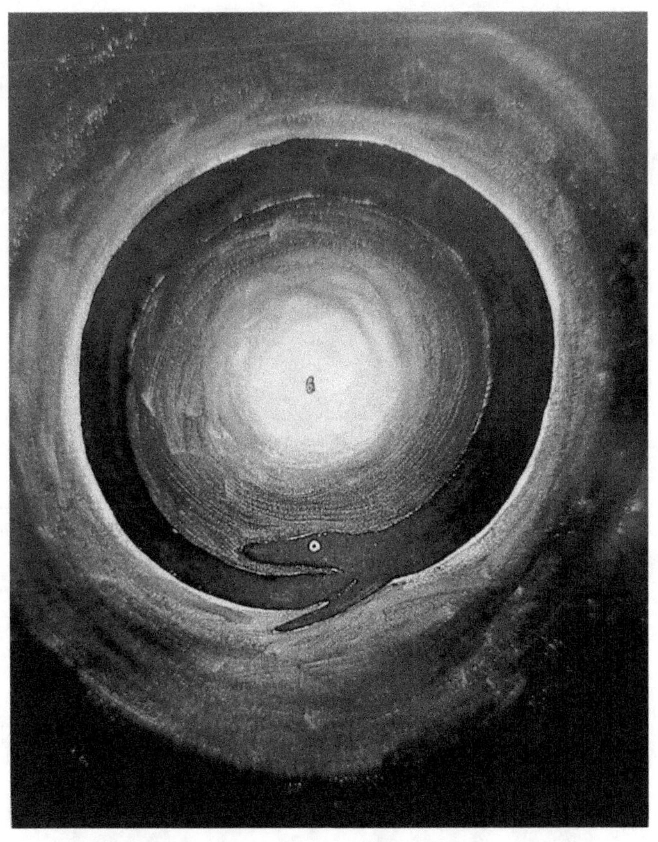

In this image, Sharon painted a round snake eating it's tail, which is known as an uroboros, which represents wholeness. It encircles red masculinity and white rebirth with the dot in the center representing her rebirth. The blue outer image, the snake, highlights the feminine aspect of the herself. She labeled the painting "Giving birth to myself."

In conclusion, Gary and Sharon were able to kill or analyze to death the parts of their egos that wanted to commit suicide. As mentioned above, it's egocide, which is symbolic suicide.

The following six healing steps begin the healing process for folks suffering from suicidal depression.

One: Acknowledgement—be honest with yourself and be aware that a problem exists.

Two: Reach out—seek help from friends, family members, doctors or clergy. Seeking help often involves individual and/or group therapy. A model for this is AA, which requires admitting your issues and getting help through counseling. See a psychiatrist, psychologist, social worker, community mental health therapist, or go to an emergency room or crisis center.

Three: Realize the way beyond is not to kill yourself, but just a part of yourself which is ego based.

Four: This is egocide, which is a meaningful alternative to suicide. Realize that the way beyond is not killing yourself, but analyzing or letting go of the suicidal part of the ego. That's why egocide allows you to live not die.

Five: The energy that went into the suicidal plan has to change and can now be utilized to create something. What to create? It will reflect the struggle and would be expressed in dreams, images, writings (poetry), change in relationship and/or vocation. As the two cases of Gary and Sharon illustrate what needed to happen.

Six: Do something creative: painting, ceramics, dance, write a poem. Find something positive and someone uplifting to spend time with.

Look in the mirror and realize that you are unique and actualize your personal myth. Analyze to death your false suicidal self, not your true self. Like and love yourself and remember—seek help and become all you can be. Take care of your body and soul.